SCHOLASTIC

P9-CSF-249

Sight Word Bingo Ladders

NEW YORK • TORONTO • LONDON • AUCKLAND • SYDNEY
MEXICO CITY • NEW DELHI • HONG KONG • BUENOS AIRES

Teaching
Resources

Written and conceived by Violet Findley
Book design by Brian LaRossa
Illustration by Doug Jones

ISBN-13: 978-0-545-22063-7 / ISBN-10: 0-545-22063-7

3 4 5 6 7 8 9 10   40   17 16 15 14 13 12 11

Contents

Introduction

Welcome to *Sight Word Bingo Ladders*! Your students will learn how to play this engaging game in an instant, but the benefit of their playing it will last a lifetime.

That's because these charming bingo ladders help children master the 300 words that most frequently appear in print (culled from the Fry List). And research shows that a mastery of these key words helps lay the foundation for long-term reading success. Why? The fact is that more than 50 percent of the text we read is made up of common, repeated words such as *the, are, be, this,* and *tell.* Thus, knowing these words by sight— that is, being able to recognize them immediately and without thought—greatly increases reading fluency and comprehension. Gaining the ability to recognize a word immediately is especially imperative in learning to read English because many of the most commonly repeated words do not follow regular phonemic rules.

Research also shows that merely relying on context and natural exposure to language, hoping children will simply "pick up" words by sight, can be a losing strategy. Most reading specialists now agree: To help jumpstart reading success, sight words should be taught directly via systematic and engaging drills. That's where these super-fun bingo games come in! They provide lots of practice with the words kids need to *internalize* in order to develop into confident, able readers. And here's more good news: The 25 games break the 300 sight words into manageable 12-word clusters, so children will never feel overwhelmed. In addition, the games enable you, as the teacher, the flexibility to choose an appropriate cluster of words to share with your students.

A few minutes a day or week is all it takes to integrate sight-word instruction into your teaching. And incorporating these lively bingo ladders into your routine is a perfect way to do just that. Treat the whole class to a quick game just before to bell rings. Or place laminated sets in a learning center for small groups or pairs to play independently. Make bingo ladders a classroom habit—and watch your students' reading skills soar!

Connection to the Language Arts Standards

The bingo games in this book are designed to support you in meeting these essential K–2 standards as outlined by the Mid-continent Research for Education and Learning (McREL) organization:

Uses the general skills and strategies of the reading process:

✓ Understands level-appropriate sight words and vocabulary.

✓ Uses phonemic analysis to decode unknown words.

✓ Uses structural analysis to decode unknown words.

Source: *Content Knowledge: A Compendium of Standards and Benchmarks for PreK–12 Education,* (4th edition). (Mid-Continent Regional Educational Laboratory, 2004)

Preparing the Games for Play

To make each of the 25 bingo games, follow these simple directions:

1. Choose the set of sight words you want to teach. Make a photocopy of the six bingo ladders, chart, and cards for that set of sight words. (Tip: For whole-class play, make duplicate copies of the ladders so that every child gets one.)

2. Cut the bingo ladders and cards apart along the dashed lines.

3. Optional: Color the ladders to make them extra appealing. Laminate the ladders, charts, and word cards to make them extra strong.

4. Purchase or prepare markers for the game, such as plastic discs, dried beans, buttons, or use the reproducible markers on pages 92–93. Also prepare a brown bag or a box with the sight word set (for example, "Sight Words 37–48") written on it.

5. Store each sight word game in a labeled manila envelope.

Components

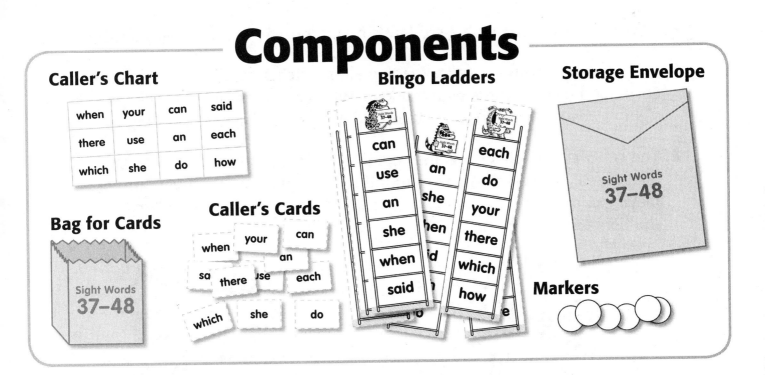

Caller's Chart

when	your	can	said
there	use	an	each
which	she	do	how

Bingo Ladders

Storage Envelope

Sight Words
37–48

Bag for Cards

Sight Words
37–48

Caller's Cards

when   your   can
                    an
sa   there   use   each
which   she   do

Markers

How to Play

The games in this book can be played by the whole class, small groups, or pairs. Here are easy instructions:

1. Choose the sight word set you want to focus on, such as sight words 1–12. (Tip: You can also use the blank templates on pages 89–91 to teach sight words that are not included in this book.)

2. Make multiple copies of the bingo ladders and distribute one to each student.

3. Give each student six markers.

4. Invite a student volunteer to act as the caller (or do so yourself). Provide the caller with the sight word chart and a brown bag or box filled with the sight word cards.

5. Ask the caller to pull out a sight word card (such as *the*), read it aloud, and place it on the sight word chart.

6. When a word appears on a student's board, he/she covers it with a marker.

7. Play continues with the caller reading aloud each sight word and students covering the sight words with markers. When a student has covered all six sight words on his/her ladder, that student shouts, "Sight Word Bingo!"

8. The caller should check the answers to make sure the student is, in fact, a winner. If so, lead students in round of applause. (NOTE: If you are playing with multiples copies of the same bingo ladder, there will be multiple winners.)

Sight Word Activities to Extend Learning

Use these quick and easy ideas to give children additional experiences with the sight words covered in this book.

Transition Time Sight Words

✓ **Lining Up:** Write sight words on index cards, creating two matching sets. Tape one set of cards to the floor where children usually line up. Place the other set in a box. Each time children need to line up, have them choose a card from the box. Then challenge children to line up by standing on the spot with the matching word. Alternatively, you can give each child a word card and challenge children to line up by putting themselves in alphabetical order.

✓ **Find a Partner:** Write pairs of matching sight words on index cards and place the cards in a bag or box. When children need to find partners for an activity, have each child pick a card. Children who picked the same card can find each other and work together.

✓ **Snack Time:** Create sight word placemats by writing target words on sheets of construction paper and laminating them or covering them with clear contact paper. Write matching words on index cards. Before snack time, place the mats on the table and give each child a random word card. Invite children to find their place at the table by finding the matching word on a placemat.

✓ **Cleaning Up:** When it's time to clean up, call out sight words one at a time. Have children spell out the word, count the number of letters, and then put away the same number of items.

✓ **Time to Go:** When it's time to pack up, avoid the cubby crush by giving each child an index card with a sight word. Invite small groups to go to their cubbies by calling out different categories, for instance: everyone whose word contains the letter *p*; everyone who has a five-letter word; everyone whose word begins with a *t*; and so on.

Sight Word Scavenger Hunt

Give each child a list of target words, a stack of old magazines, a sheet of construction paper, scissors, and glue. Then have children hunt through the magazines for the words on their list. Each time they find a word, they can cut it out and glue it on the paper. When finished, children will have a sight word collage, most likely filled with lots of different fonts and colors.

Sight Word Tic-Tac-Toe

Draw a tic tac toe grid on the board and divide the class into two teams, X's and O's. Fill each space in the grid with a sight word. The game is played just like regular tic-tac-toe, with members of each team choosing a space to cover. In order to mark the space with an X or an O, the team member must read the word in that space correctly. The team that gets three X's or O's in a row wins the game.

Shake-a-Word

To prepare this game, get a clean, empty egg carton and small self-stick labels. Write different sight words on 12 labels and stick one in each cup of the carton. Then place a number cube inside the carton. In groups of two to four, have children play the game as follows. The first player closes the carton and shakes it. He or she then opens up the carton and notes what number is facing up on the cube. The child then removes the cube and reads the sight word that's printed in the cup in which the cube landed. If the child reads the word correctly, he or she earns the number of points shown on the cube. Then it is the next player's turn. Children can play for a set number of rounds or as time permits.

Sentence-Builder Hangman

This version of "hangman" reinforces both spelling and how words are used in context. Choose a "mystery" sight word and build a sentence around it, writing blanks for the letters of the target word. For instance, for the word *around*, you might write: "The dog chased the cat _ _ _ _ _ _ the yard." Just like regular hangman, children guess one letter at a time. If the letter appears in the word, write it on the appropriate space. If not, add one body part to the "hangman." Children try to solve the word before the body is complete!

Go Fish

Create a deck of cards by writing 26 sight words on separate index cards. Write each word twice on each card, and cut the cards in half to make a deck of 52 cards. Children can play the game in groups of three to six. Each player gets five cards, and the remaining cards are placed facedown in the middle. The first player chooses a word from his or her hand and asks another player for the matching word card. If the player has the card, he or she hands it over. If not, that player says, "Go fish," and the first player picks the top card from the middle deck. If the drawn card makes a pair, the player places the pair on the table. If not, the player keeps the card and it is the next player's turn. Play continues until one player runs out of cards or the deck in the middle is used up.

First 300 Sight Words*

1. the	30. words	59. these	88. oil	117. after
2. of	31. but	60. so	89. sit	118. things
3. and	32. not	61. some	90. now	119. our
4. a	33. what	62. her	91. find	120. just
5. to	34. all	63. would	92. long	121. name
6. in	35. were	64. make	93. down	122. good
7. is	36. we	65. like	94. day	123. sentence
8. you	37. when	66. him	95. did	124. man
9. that	38. your	67. into	96. get	125. think
10. it	39. can	68. time	97. come	126. say
11. he	40. said	69. has	98. made	127. great
12. was	41. there	70. look	99. may	128. where
13. for	42. use	71. two	100. part	129. help
14. on	43. an	72. more	101. over	130. through
15. are	44. each	73. write	102. new	131. much
16. as	45. which	74. go	103. sound	132. before
17. with	46. she	75. see	104. take	133. line
18. his	47. do	76. number	105. only	134. right
19. they	48. how	77. no	106. little	135. too
20. I	49. their	78. way	107. work	136. means
21. at	50. if	79. could	108. know	137. old
22. be	51. will	80. people	109. place	138. any
23. this	52. up	81. my	110. years	139. same
24. have	53. other	82. than	111. live	140. tell
25. from	54. about	83. first	112. me	141. boy
26. or	55. out	84. water	113. back	142. follow
27. one	56. many	85. been	114. give	143. came
28. had	57. then	86. called	115. most	144. want
29. by	58. them	87. who	116. very	145. show

* These words are from the Fry Word List.

146. also	**177.** kind	**208.** below	**239.** example	**270.** book
147. around	**178.** hand	**209.** country	**240.** begin	**271.** hear
148. form	**179.** picture	**210.** plant	**241.** life	**272.** stop
149. three	**180.** again	**211.** last	**242.** always	**273.** without
150. small	**181.** change	**212.** school	**243.** those	**274.** second
151. set	**182.** off	**213.** father	**244.** both	**275.** late
152. put	**183.** play	**214.** keep	**245.** paper	**276.** miss
153. end	**184.** spell	**215.** tree	**246.** together	**277.** idea
154. does	**185.** air	**216.** never	**247.** got	**278.** enough
155. another	**186.** away	**217.** start	**248.** group	**279.** eat
156. well	**187.** animal	**218.** city	**249.** often	**280.** face
157. large	**188.** house	**219.** earth	**250.** run	**281.** watch
158. must	**189.** point	**220.** eyes	**251.** important	**282.** far
159. big	**190.** page	**221.** light	**252.** until	**283.** Indian
160. even	**191.** letter	**222.** though	**253.** children	**284.** real
161. such	**192.** mother	**223.** head	**254.** side	**285.** almost
162. because	**193.** answer	**224.** under	**255.** feet	**286.** let
163. turn	**194.** found	**225.** story	**256.** car	**287.** above
164. here	**195.** study	**226.** saw	**257.** mile	**288.** girl
165. why	**196.** still	**227.** left	**258.** night	**289.** sometimes
166. ask	**197.** learn	**228.** don't	**259.** walk	**290.** mountains
167. went	**198.** should	**229.** few	**260.** white	**291.** cut
168. men	**199.** America	**230.** while	**261.** sea	**292.** young
169. read	**200.** world	**231.** along	**262.** began	**293.** talk
170. need	**201.** high	**232.** might	**263.** grow	**294.** soon
171. land	**202.** every	**233.** close	**264.** took	**295.** list
172. different	**203.** near	**234.** something	**265.** river	**296.** song
173. home	**204.** add	**235.** seem	**266.** four	**297.** being
174. us	**205.** food	**236.** next	**267.** carry	**298.** leave
175. move	**206.** between	**237.** hard	**268.** state	**299.** family
176. try	**207.** own	**238.** open	**269.** once	**300.** it's

Sight Word Bingo Ladders

CALLER'S CHART

the	of	and	a
to	in	is	you
that	it	he	was

CALLER'S CARDS

the	of	and	a
to	in	is	you
that	it	he	was

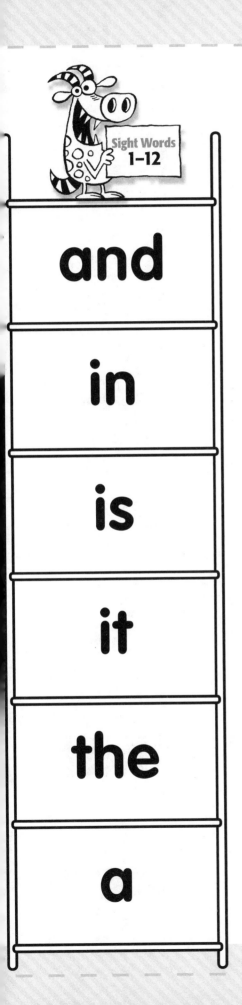

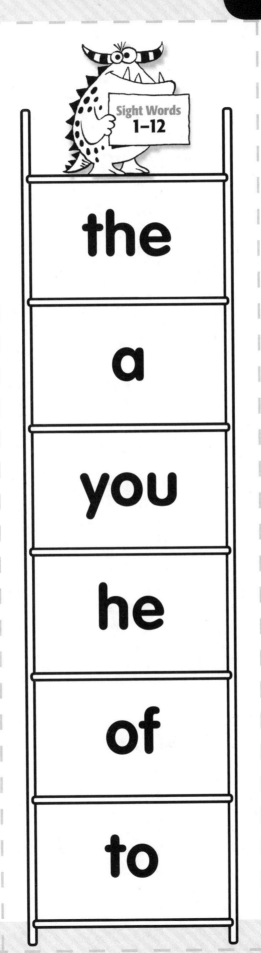

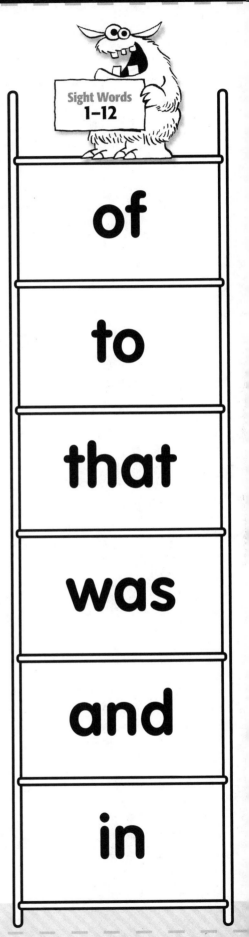

and	the	of
in	a	to
is	you	that
it	he	was
the	of	and
a	to	in

LADDERS

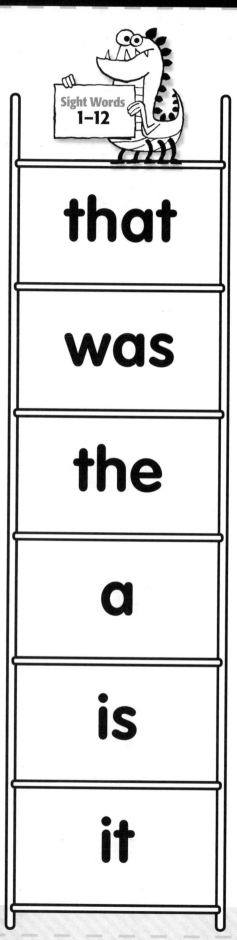

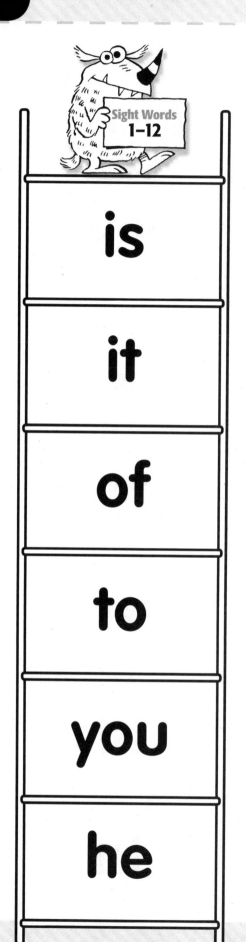

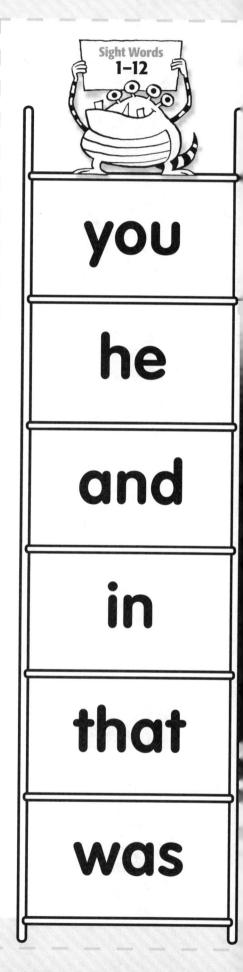

that	is	you
was	it	he
the	of	and
a	to	in
is	you	that
it	he	was

CALLER'S CHART

for	on	are	as
with	his	they	I
at	be	this	have

CALLER'S CARDS

for	on	are	as
with	his	they	I
at	be	this	have

LADDERS

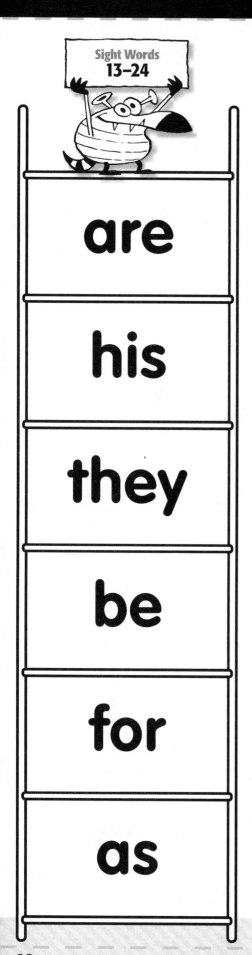

are
his
they
be
for
as

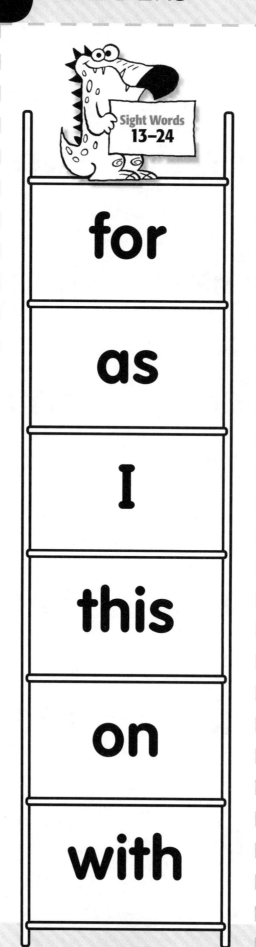

for
as
I
this
on
with

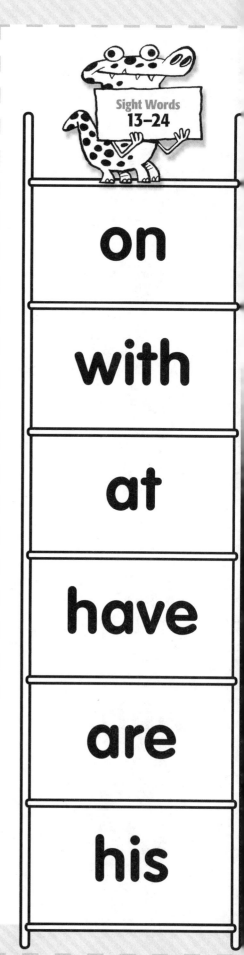

on
with
at
have
are
his

at

have

for

as

they

be

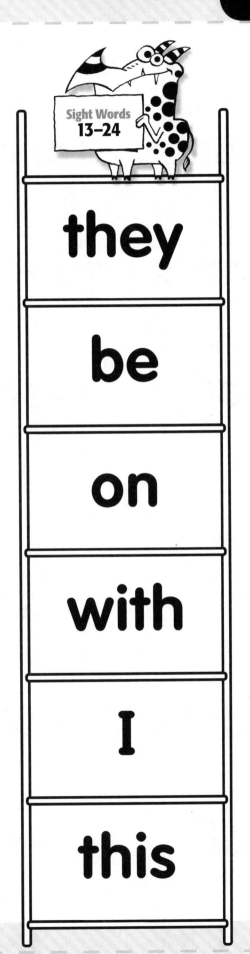

they

be

on

with

I

this

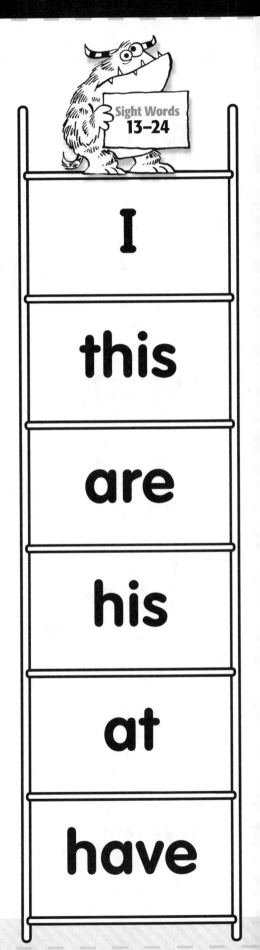

I

this

are

his

at

have

CALLER'S CHART

from	or	one	had
by	words	but	not
what	all	were	we

CALLER'S CARDS

from	or	one	had
by	words	but	not
what	all	were	we

one	from	or
words	had	by
but	not	what
all	were	we
from	or	one
had	by	words

LADDERS

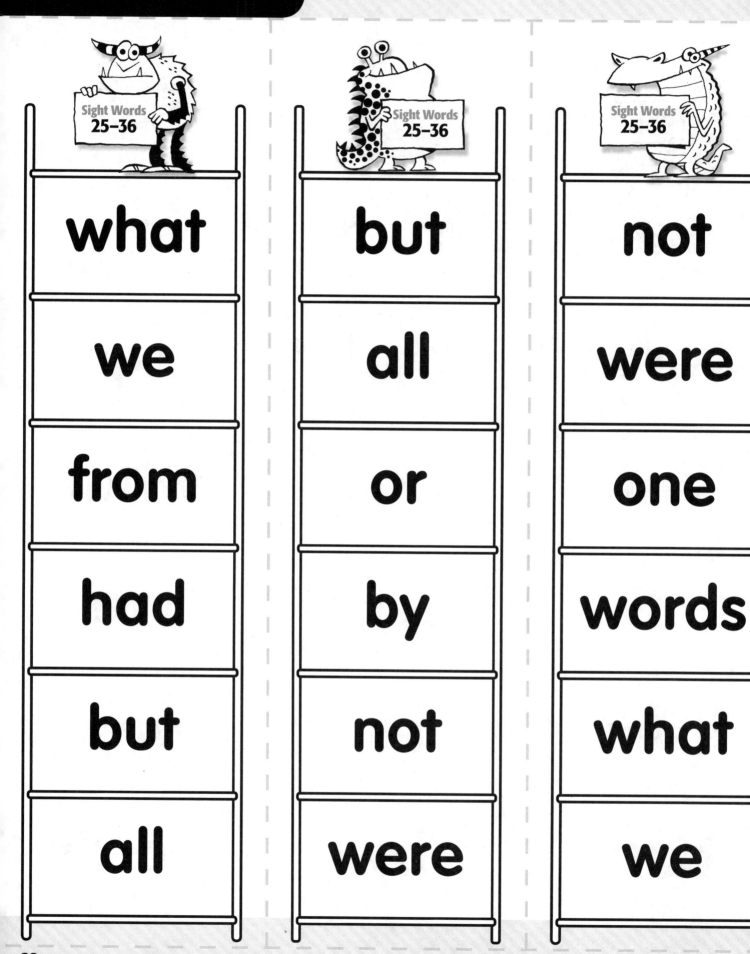

what	but	not
we	all	were
from	or	one
had	by	words
but	not	what
all	were	we

CALLER'S CHART

when	your	can	said
there	use	an	each
which	she	do	how

CALLER'S CARDS

when	your	can	said
there	use	an	each
which	she	do	how

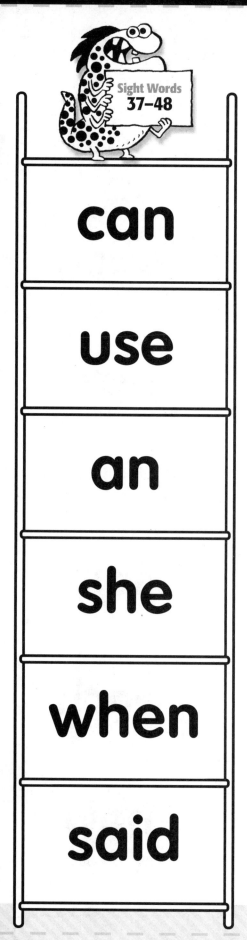

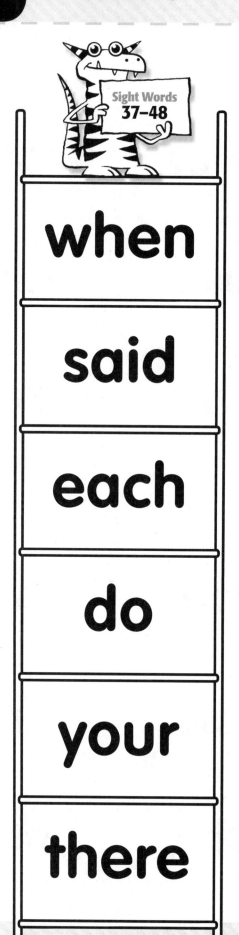

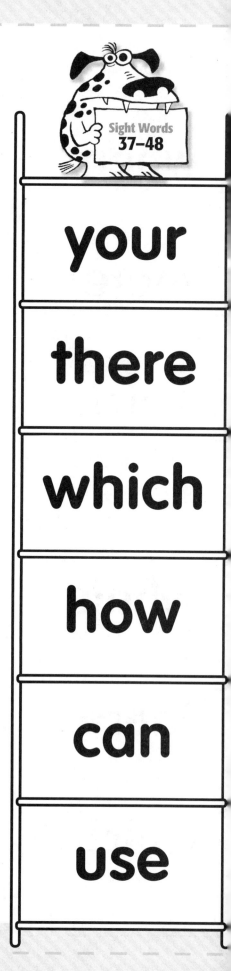

can	when	your
use	said	there
an	each	which
she	do	how
when	your	can
said	there	use

an	each	which
she	do	how
when	your	can
said	there	use
each	which	an
do	how	she

CALLER'S CHART

their	if	will	up
other	about	out	many
then	them	these	so

CALLER'S CARDS

their	if	will	up
other	about	out	many
then	them	these	so

Sight Words 49–60

Sight Words 49–60

Sight Words 49–60

if	will	their
other	about	up
out	many	then
them	these	so
their	if	will
up	other	about

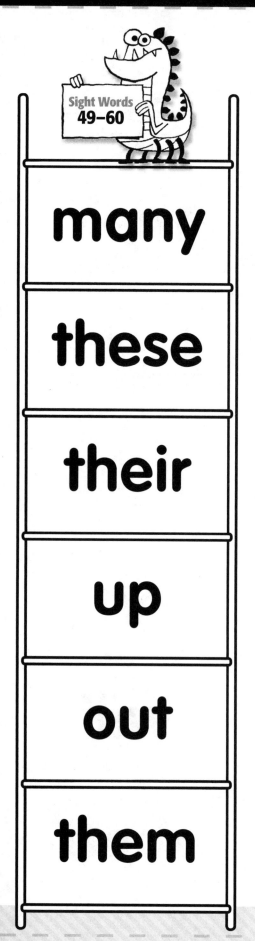

many
these
their
up
out
them

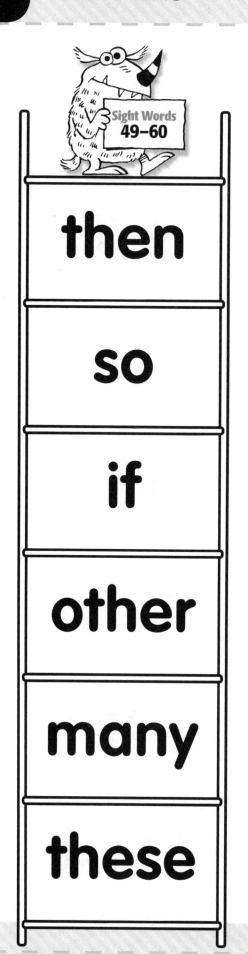

then
so
if
other
many
these

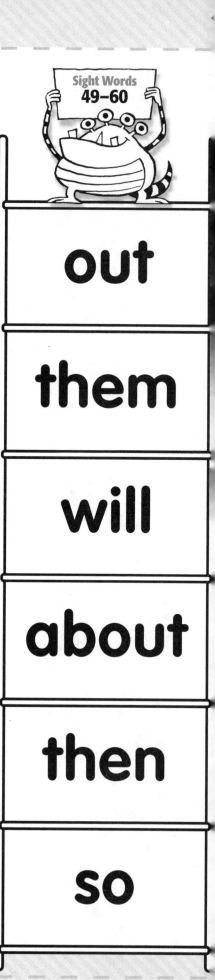

out
them
will
about
then
so

some	her	would	make
like	him	into	time
has	look	two	more

CALLER'S CARDS

some	her	would	make
like	him	into	time
has	look	two	more

LADDERS

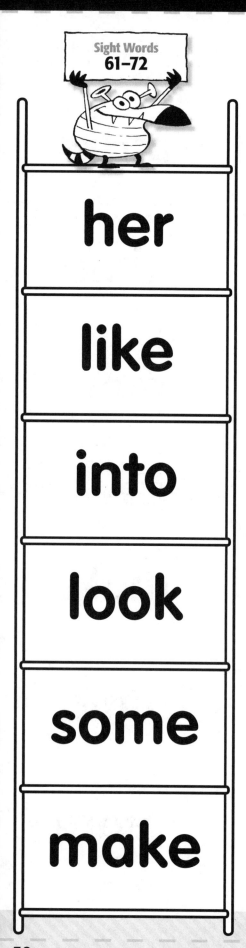

her
like
into
look
some
make

would
him
time
two
her
like

some
make
has
more
would
him

Sight Words
61–72

Sight Words
61–72

Sight Words
61–72

time	has	into
two	more	look
some	her	would
make	like	him
into	time	has
look	two	more

CALLER'S CHART

write	go	see	number
no	way	could	people
my	than	first	water

CALLER'S CARDS

write	go	see	number
no	way	could	people
my	than	first	water

go	see	write
no	way	number
could	people	my
than	first	water
write	go	see
number	no	way

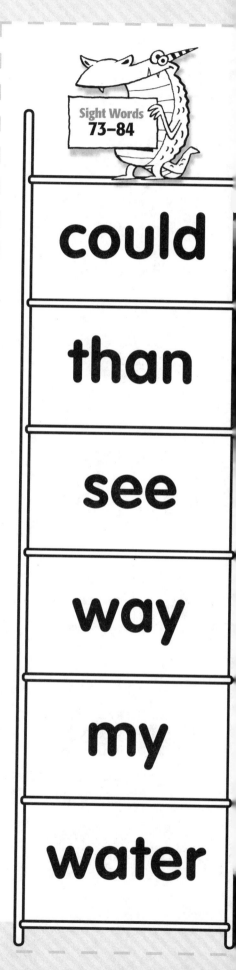

people	my	could
first	water	than
write	go	see
number	no	way
could	people	my
than	first	water

CALLER'S CHART

been	called	who	oil
sit	now	find	long
down	day	did	get

CALLER'S CARDS

been	called	who	oil
sit	now	find	long
down	day	did	get

called	who	been
sit	now	oil
find	long	down
day	did	get
been	called	who
oil	sit	now

long	down	find
did	get	day
been	called	who
oil	sit	now
find	long	down
day	did	get

CALLER'S CHART

come	made	may	part
over	new	sound	take
only	little	work	know

CALLER'S CARDS

come	made	may	part
over	new	sound	take
only	little	work	know

Sight Words
97–108

Sight Words
97–108

Sight Words
97–108

made	may	come
over	new	part
sound	take	only
little	work	know
come	made	may
part	over	new

take	only	sound
work	know	little
come	made	may
part	over	new
sound	take	only
little	work	know

CALLER'S CHART

place	years	live	me
back	give	most	very
after	things	our	just

CALLER'S CARDS

place	years	live	me
back	give	most	very
after	things	our	just

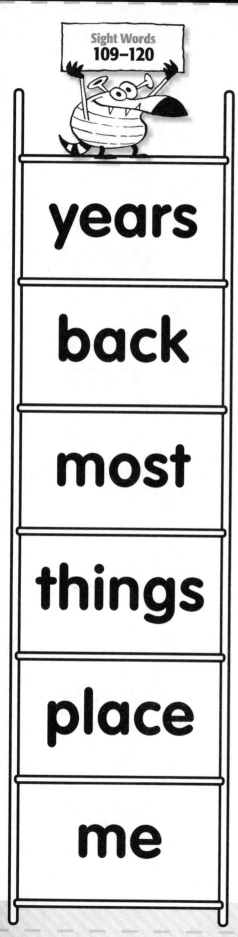

years

back

most

things

place

me

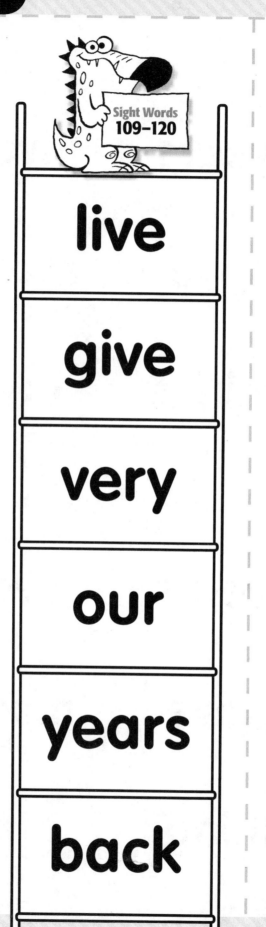

live

give

very

our

years

back

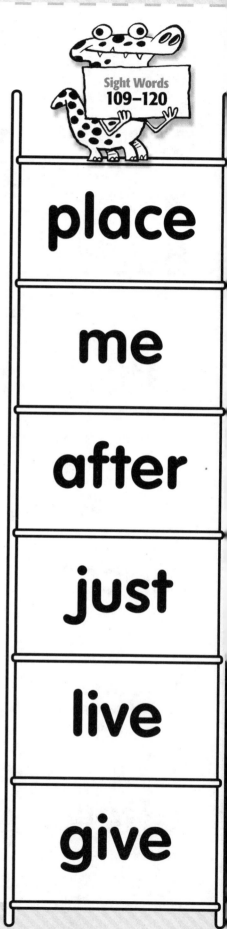

place

me

after

just

live

give

42

Sight Words 109–120

Sight Words 109–120

Sight Words 109–120

very	after	most
our	just	things
place	years	live
me	back	give
most	very	after
things	our	just

CALLER'S CHART

name	good	sentence	man
think	say	great	where
help	through	much	before

CALLER'S CARDS

name	good	sentence	man
think	say	great	where
help	through	much	before

good	sentence	name
think	say	man
great	where	help
through	much	before
name	good	sentence
man	think	say

where	help	great
much	before	through
name	good	sentence
man	think	say
great	where	help
through	much	before

CALLER'S CHART

line	right	too	means
old	any	same	tell
boy	follow	came	want

CALLER'S CARDS

line	right	too	means
old	any	same	tell
boy	follow	came	want

right	too	line
old	any	means
same	tell	boy
follow	came	want
line	right	too
means	old	any

tell	boy	same
came	want	follow
line	right	too
means	old	any
same	tell	boy
follow	came	want

CALLER'S CHART

show	also	around	form
three	small	set	put
end	does	another	well

CALLER'S CARDS

show	also	around	form
three	small	set	put
end	does	another	well

also	around	show
three	small	form
set	put	end
does	another	well
show	also	around
form	three	small

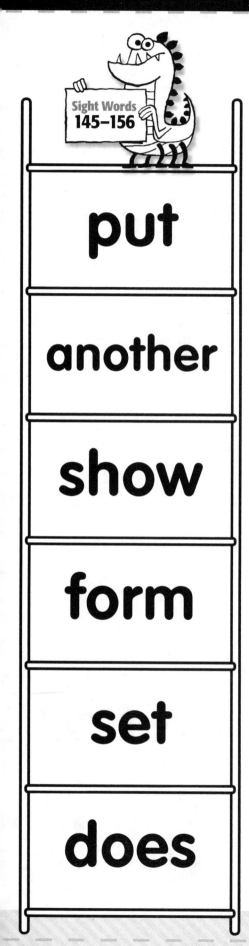

put

another

show

form

set

does

end

well

also

three

put

another

set

does

around

small

end

well

CALLER'S CHART

large	must	big	even
such	because	turn	here
why	ask	went	men

CALLER'S CARDS

large	must	big	even
such	because	turn	here
why	ask	went	men

must	big	large
such	because	even
turn	here	why
ask	went	men
large	must	big
even	such	because

here	why	turn
went	men	ask
large	must	big
even	such	because
turn	here	why
ask	went	men

CALLER'S CHART

read	need	land	different
home	us	move	try
kind	hand	picture	again

CALLER'S CARDS

read	need	land	different
home	us	move	try
kind	hand	picture	again

Sight Words
169–180

Sight Words
169–180

Sight Words
169–180

need	land	read
home	us	different
move	try	kind
hand	picture	again
read	need	land
different	home	us

try	kind	move
picture	again	hand
read	need	land
different	home	us
move	try	kind
hand	picture	again

CALLER'S CHART

change	off	play	spell
air	away	animal	house
point	page	letter	mother

CALLER'S CARDS

change	off	play	spell
air	away	animal	house
point	page	letter	mother

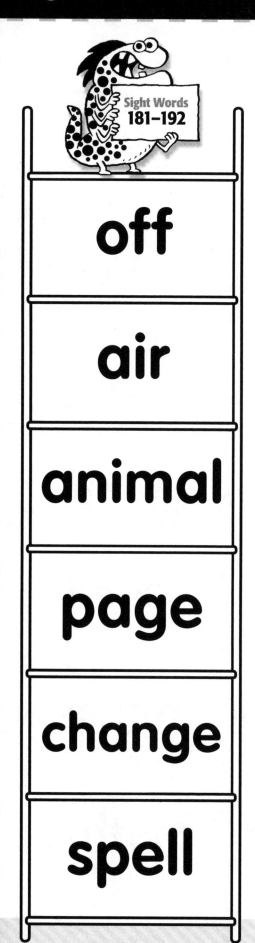

air

animal

page

change

spell

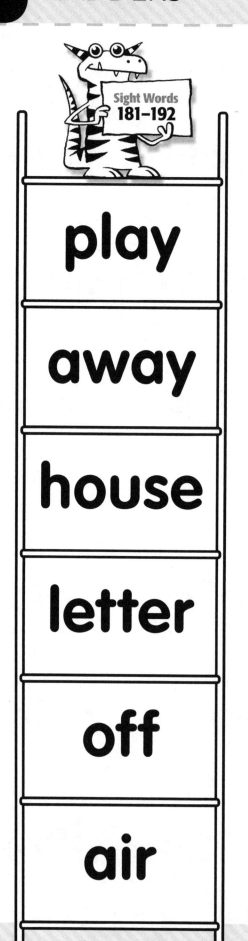

play

away

house

letter

off

air

change

spell

point

mother

play

away

| house |
| letter |
| change |
| spell |
| animal |
| page |

| point |
| mother |
| off |
| air |
| house |
| letter |

| animal |
| page |
| play |
| away |
| point |
| mother |

CALLER'S CHART

answer	found	study	still
learn	should	America	world
high	every	near	add

CALLER'S CARDS

answer	found	study	still
learn	should	America	world
high	every	near	add

found	study	answer
learn	should	still
America	world	high
every	near	add
answer	found	study
still	learn	should

world	high	America
near	add	every
answer	found	study
still	learn	should
America	world	high
every	near	add

CALLER'S CHART

food	between	own	below
country	plant	last	school
father	keep	tree	never

CALLER'S CARDS

food	between	own	below
country	plant	last	school
father	keep	tree	never

between	own	food
country	plant	below
last	school	father
keep	tree	never
food	between	own
below	country	last

school	father	food
tree	never	father
keep	between	own
below	country	plant
never	keep	school
plant	last	tree

CALLER'S CHART

start	city	earth	eyes
light	though	head	under
story	saw	left	don't

CALLER'S CARDS

start	city	earth	eyes
light	though	head	under
story	saw	left	don't

Sight Words
217–228

city	earth	start
light	though	eyes
head	under	story
saw	left	don't
start	city	earth
eyes	light	though

under	story	head
left	don't	saw
start	city	earth
eyes	light	though
head	under	story
saw	left	don't

CALLER'S CHART

few	while	along	might
close	something	seem	next
hard	open	example	begin

CALLER'S CARDS

few	while	along	might
close	something	seem	next
hard	open	example	begin

while	along	few
close	something	might
seem	next	hard
open	example	begin
few	while	along
might	close	something

next	**hard**	**seem**
example	**begin**	**open**
few	**while**	**along**
might	**close**	something
seem	**next**	**hard**
open	example	**begin**

CALLER'S CHART

life	always	those	both
paper	together	got	group
often	run	important	until

CALLER'S CARDS

life	always	those	both
paper	together	got	group
often	run	important	until

always	those	life
paper	together	both
got	group	often
run	important	until
life	always	those
both	paper	together

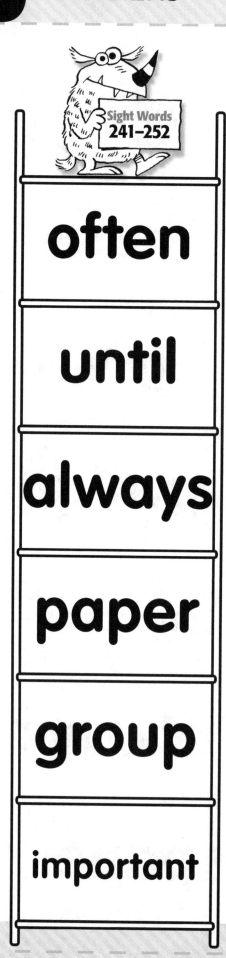

group	often	got
important	until	run
life	always	those
both	paper	together
got	group	often
run	important	until

CALLER'S CHART

children	side	feet	car
mile	night	walk	white
sea	began	grow	took

CALLER'S CARDS

children	side	feet	car
mile	night	walk	white
sea	began	grow	took

side

mile

walk

began

children

car

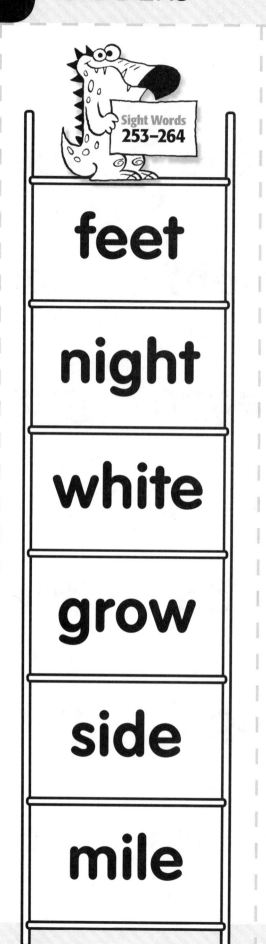

feet

night

white

grow

side

mile

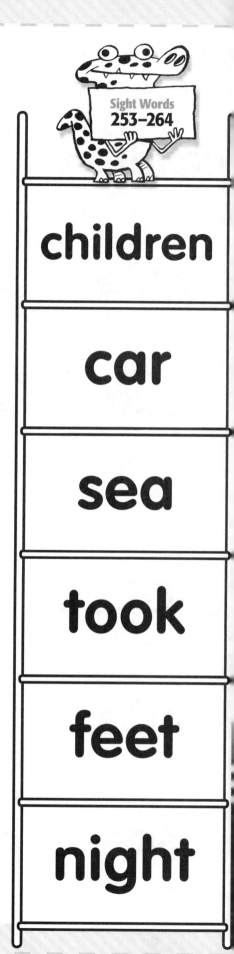

children

car

sea

took

feet

night

white	sea	walk
grow	took	began
children	side	feet
car	mile	night
walk	white	sea
began	grow	took

CALLER'S CHART

river	four	carry	state
once	book	hear	stop
without	second	late	miss

CALLER'S CARDS

river	four	carry	state
once	book	hear	stop
without	second	late	miss

four	carry	river
once	book	state
hear	stop	without
second	late	miss
river	four	carry
state	once	book

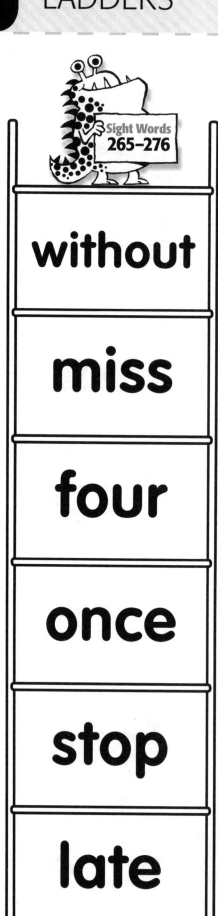

Ladder 1

stop

late

river

state

hear

second

Ladder 2

without

miss

four

once

stop

late

Ladder 3

hear

second

carry

book

without

miss

Sight Words 265–276

Sight Words 265–276

Sight Words 265–276

CALLER'S CHART

idea	enough	eat	face
watch	far	Indian	real
almost	let	above	girl

CALLER'S CARDS

idea	enough	eat	face
watch	far	Indian	real
almost	let	above	girl

enough	eat	idea
watch	far	face
Indian	real	almost
let	above	girl
idea	enough	eat
face	watch	far

real	almost	let
above	girl	Indian
Indian	enough	eat
face	watch	far
almost	idea	real
girl	let	above

CALLER'S CHART

sometimes	mountains	cut	young
talk	soon	list	song
being	leave	family	it's

CALLER'S CARDS

sometimes	mountains	cut	young
talk	soon	list	song
being	leave	family	it's

Sight Words 289–300

mountains	cut	sometimes
talk	soon	young
list	song	being
leave	family	it's
sometimes	mountains	cut
young	talk	soon

song

family

sometimes

young

list

leave

being

it's

mountains

talk

song

family

list

leave

cut

soon

being

it's

CALLER'S CHART

CALLER'S CARDS

Reproducible Markers (Circles)

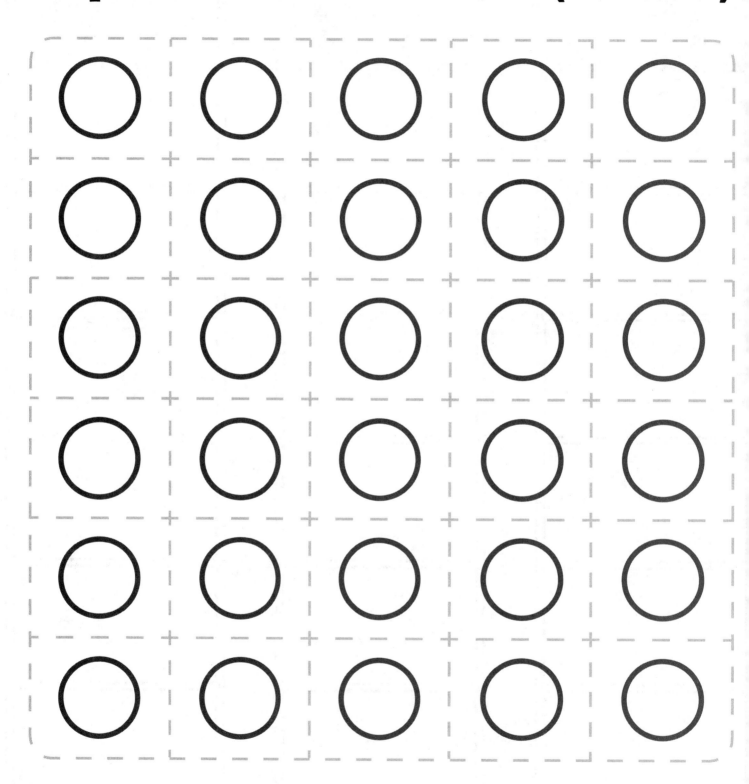

Reproducible Markers (Stars)

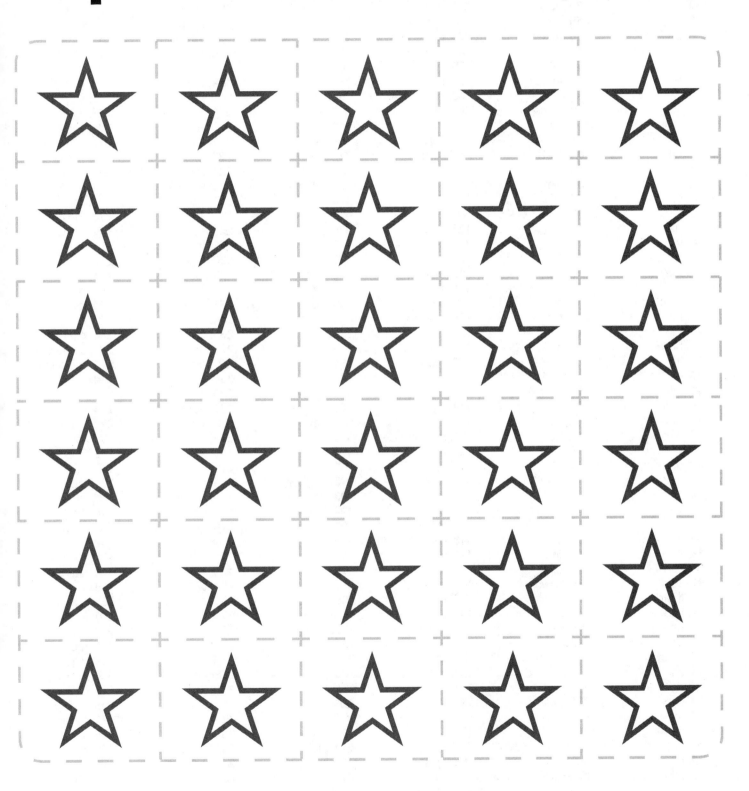

First 1,000 Sight Words*

1. the	54. about	107. work	160. even	213. father	266. four
2. of	55. out	108. know	161. such	214. keep	267. carry
3. and	56. many	109. place	162. because	215. tree	268. state
4. a	57. then	110. years	163. turn	216. never	269. once
5. to	58. them	111. live	164. here	217. start	270. book
6. in	59. these	112. me	165. why	218. city	271. hear
7. is	60. so	113. back	166. ask	219. earth	272. stop
8. you	61. some	114. give	167. went	220. eyes	273. without
9. that	62. her	115. most	168. men	221. light	274. second
10. it	63. would	116. very	169. read	222. though	275. late
11. he	64. make	117. after	170. need	223. head	276. miss
12. was	65. like	118. things	171. land	224. under	277. idea
13. for	66. him	119. our	172. different	225. story	278. enough
14. on	67. into	120. just	173. home	226. saw	279. eat
15. are	68. time	121. name	174. us	227. left	280. face
16. as	69. has	122. good	175. move	228. don't	281. watch
17. with	70. look	123. sentence	176. try	229. few	282. far
18. his	71. two	124. man	177. kind	230. while	283. Indian
19. they	72. more	125. think	178. hand	231. along	284. real
20. I	73. write	126. say	179. picture	232. might	285. almost
21. at	74. go	127. great	180. again	233. close	286. let
22. be	75. see	128. where	181. change	234. something	287. above
23. this	76. number	129. help	182. off	235. seem	288. girl
24. have	77. no	130. through	183. play	236. next	289. sometimes
25. from	78. way	131. much	184. spell	237. hard	290. mountains
26. or	79. could	132. before	185. air	238. open	291. cut
27. one	80. people	133. line	186. away	239. example	292. young
28. had	81. my	134. right	187. animal	240. begin	293. talk
29. by	82. than	135. too	188. house	241. life	294. soon
30. words	83. first	136. means	189. point	242. always	295. list
31. but	84. water	137. old	190. page	243. those	296. song
32. not	85. been	138. any	191. letter	244. both	297. being
33. what	86. called	139. same	192. mother	245. paper	298. leave
34. all	87. who	140. tell	193. answer	246. together	299. family
35. were	88. oil	141. boy	194. found	247. got	300. it's
36. we	89. sit	142. follow	195. study	248. group	301. body
37. when	90. now	143. came	196. still	249. often	302. music
38. your	91. find	144. want	197. learn	250. run	303. color
39. can	92. long	145. show	198. should	251. important	304. stand
40. said	93. down	146. also	199. America	252. until	305. sun
41. there	94. day	147. around	200. world	253. children	306. questions
42. use	95. did	148. form	201. high	254. side	307. fish
43. an	96. get	149. three	202. every	255. feet	308. area
44. each	97. come	150. small	203. near	256. car	309. mark
45. which	98. made	151. set	204. add	257. mile	310. dog
46. she	99. may	152. put	205. food	258. night	311. horse
47. do	100. part	153. end	206. between	259. walk	312. birds
48. how	101. over	154. does	207. own	260. white	313. problem
49. their	102. new	155. another	208. below	261. sea	314. complete
50. if	103. sound	156. well	209. country	262. began	315. room
51. will	104. take	157. large	210. plant	263. grow	316. knew
52. up	105. only	158. must	211. last	264. took	317. since
53. other	106. little	159. big	212. school	265. river	318. ever

* These words are from the Fry Word List.

319. piece	**376.** busy	**433.** class	**490.** size	**547.** summer	**604.** appear
320. told	**377.** pulled	**434.** note	**491.** dark	**548.** wall	**605.** metal
321. usually	**378.** draw	**435.** nothing	**492.** ball	**549.** forest	**606.** son
322. didn't	**379.** voice	**436.** rest	**493.** material	**550.** probably	**607.** either
323. friends	**380.** seen	**437.** carefully	**494.** special	**551.** legs	**608.** ice
324. easy	**381.** cold	**438.** scientists	**495.** heavy	**552.** sat	**609.** sleep
325. heard	**382.** cried	**439.** inside	**496.** fine	**553.** main	**610.** village
326. order	**383.** plan	**440.** wheels	**497.** pair	**554.** winter	**611.** factors
327. red	**384.** notice	**441.** stay	**498.** circle	**555.** wide	**612.** result
328. door	**385.** south	**442.** green	**499.** include	**556.** written	**613.** jumped
329. sure	**386.** sing	**443.** known	**500.** built	**557.** length	**614.** snow
330. become	**387.** war	**444.** island	**501.** can't	**558.** reason	**615.** ride
331. top	**388.** ground	**445.** week	**502.** matter	**559.** kept	**616.** care
332. ship	**389.** fall	**446.** less	**503.** square	**560.** interest	**617.** floor
333. across	**390.** king	**447.** machine	**504.** syllables	**561.** arms	**618.** hill
334. today	**391.** town	**448.** base	**505.** perhaps	**562.** brother	**619.** pushed
335. during	**392.** I'll	**449.** ago	**506.** bill	**563.** race	**620.** baby
336. short	**393.** unit	**450.** stood	**507.** felt	**564.** present	**621.** buy
337. better	**394.** figure	**451.** plane	**508.** suddenly	**565.** beautiful	**622.** century
338. best	**395.** certain	**452.** system	**509.** test	**566.** store	**623.** outside
339. however	**396.** field	**453.** behind	**510.** direction	**567.** job	**624.** everything
340. low	**397.** travel	**454.** ran	**511.** center	**568.** edge	**625.** tall
341. hours	**398.** wood	**455.** round	**512.** farmers	**569.** past	**626.** already
342. black	**399.** fire	**456.** boat	**513.** ready	**570.** sign	**627.** instead
343. products	**400.** upon	**457.** game	**514.** anything	**571.** record	**628.** phrase
344. happened	**401.** done	**458.** force	**515.** divided	**572.** finished	**629.** soil
345. whole	**402.** English	**459.** brought	**516.** general	**573.** discovered	**630.** bed
346. measure	**403.** road	**460.** understand	**517.** energy	**574.** wild	**631.** copy
347. remember	**404.** halt	**461.** warm	**518.** subject	**575.** happy	**632.** free
348. early	**405.** ten	**462.** common	**519.** Europe	**576.** beside	**633.** hope
349. waves	**406.** fly	**463.** bring	**520.** moon	**577.** gone	**634.** spring
350. reached	**407.** gave	**464.** explain	**521.** region	**578.** sky	**635.** case
351. listen	**408.** box	**465.** dry	**522.** return	**579.** glass	**636.** laughed
352. wind	**409.** finally	**466.** though	**523.** believe	**580.** million	**637.** nation
353. rock	**410.** wait	**467.** language	**524.** dance	**581.** west	**638.** quite
354. space	**411.** correct	**468.** shape	**525.** members	**582.** lay	**639.** type
355. covered	**412.** oh	**469.** deep	**526.** picked	**583.** weather	**640.** themselves
356. fast	**413.** quickly	**470.** thousands	**527.** simple	**584.** root	**641.** temperature
357. several	**414.** person	**471.** yes	**528.** cells	**585.** instruments	**642.** bright
358. hold	**415.** became	**472.** clear	**529.** paint	**586.** meet	**643.** lead
359. himself	**416.** shown	**473.** equation	**530.** mind	**587.** third	**644.** everyone
360. toward	**417.** minutes	**474.** yet	**531.** love	**588.** months	**645.** method
361. five	**418.** strong	**475.** government	**532.** cause	**589.** paragraph	**646.** section
362. step	**419.** verb	**476.** filled	**533.** rain	**590.** raised	**647.** lake
363. morning	**420.** stars	**477.** heat	**534.** exercise	**591.** represent	**648.** consonant
364. passed	**421.** front	**478.** full	**535.** eggs	**592.** soft	**649.** within
365. vowel	**422.** feel	**479.** hot	**536.** train	**593.** whether	**650.** dictionary
366. true	**423.** fact	**480.** check	**537.** blue	**594.** clothes	**651.** hair
367. hundred	**424.** inches	**481.** object	**538.** wish	**595.** flowers	**652.** age
368. against	**425.** street	**482.** bread	**539.** drop	**596.** shall	**653.** amount
369. pattern	**426.** decided	**483.** rule	**540.** developed	**597.** teacher	**654.** scale
370. numeral	**427.** contain	**484.** among	**541.** window	**598.** held	**655.** pounds
371. table	**428.** course	**485.** noun	**542.** difference	**599.** describe	**656.** although
372. north	**429.** surface	**486.** power	**543.** distance	**600.** drive	**657.** per
373. slowly	**430.** produce	**487.** cannot	**544.** heart	**601.** cross	**658.** broken
374. money	**431.** building	**488.** able	**545.** site	**602.** speak	**659.** moment
375. map	**432.** ocean	**489.** six	**546.** sum	**603.** solve	**660.** tiny

661. possible
662. gold
663. milk
664. quiet
665. natural
666. lot
667. stone
668. act
669. build
670. middle
671. speed
672. count
673. cat
674. someone
675. sail
676. rolled
677. bear
678. wonder
679. smiled
680. angle
681. fraction
682. Africa
683. killed
684. melody
685. bottom
686. trip
687. hole
688. poor
689. let's
690. fight
691. surprise
692. French
693. died
694. beat
695. exactly
696. remain
697. dress
698. iron
699. couldn't
700. fingers
701. row
702. least
703. catch
704. climbed
705. wrote
706. shouted
707. continued
708. itself
709. else
710. plains
711. gas
712. England
713. burning
714. design
715. joined
716. foot
717. law

718. ears
719. grass
720. you're
721. grew
722. skin
723. valley
724. cents
725. key
726. president
727. brown
728. trouble
729. cool
730. cloud
731. lost
732. sent
733. symbols
734. wear
735. bad
736. save
737. experiment
738. engine
739. alone
740. drawing
741. east
742. pay
743. single
744. touch
745. information
746. express
747. mouth
748. yard
749. equal
750. decimal
751. yourself
752. control
753. practice
754. report
755. straight
756. rise
757. statement
758. stick
759. party
760. seeds
761. supposed
762. woman
763. coast
764. bank
765. period
766. wire
767. choose
768. clean
769. visit
770. bit
771. whose
772. received
773. garden
774. please

775. strange
776. caught
777. fell
778. team
779. God
780. captain
781. direct
782. ring
783. serve
784. child
785. desert
786. increase
787. history
788. cost
789. maybe
790. business
791. separate
792. break
793. uncle
794. hunting
795. flow
796. lady
797. students
798. human
799. art
800. feeling
801. supply
802. corner
803. electric
804. insects
805. crops
806. tone
807. hit
808. sand
809. doctor
810. provide
811. thus
812. won't
813. cook
814. bones
815. tail
816. board
817. modern
818. compound
819. mine
820. wasn't
821. fit
822. addition
823. belong
824. safe
825. soldiers
826. guess
827. silent
828. trade
829. rather
830. compare
831. crowd

832. poem
833. enjoy
834. elements
835. indicate
836. except
837. expect
838. flat
839. seven
840. interesting
841. sense
842. string
843. blow
844. famous
845. value
846. wings
847. movement
848. pole
849. exciting
850. branches
851. thick
852. blood
853. lie
854. spot
855. bell
856. fun
857. loud
858. consider
859. suggested
860. thin
861. position
862. entered
863. fruit
864. tied
865. rich
866. dollars
867. send
868. sight
869. chief
870. Japanese
871. stream
872. planets
873. rhythm
874. eight
875. science
876. major
877. observe
878. tube
879. necessary
880. weight
881. meat
882. lifted
883. process
884. army
885. hat
886. property
887. particular
888. swim

889. terms
890. current
891. park
892. sell
893. shoulder
894. industry
895. wash
896. block
897. spread
898. cattle
899. wife
900. sharp
901. company
902. radio
903. we'll
904. action
905. capital
906. factories
907. settled
908. yellow
909. isn't
910. southern
911. truck
912. fair
913. printed
914. wouldn't
915. ahead
916. chance
917. born
918. level
919. triangle
920. molecules
921. France
922. repeated
923. column
924. western
925. church
926. sister
927. oxygen
928. plural
929. various
930. agreed
931. opposite
932. wrong
933. chart
934. prepared
935. pretty
936. solution
937. fresh
938. shop
939. suffix
940. especially
941. shoes
942. actually
943. nose
944. afraid
945. dead

946. sugar
947. adjective
948. fig
949. office
950. huge
951. gun
952. similar
953. death
954. score
955. forward
956. stretched
957. experience
958. rose
959. allow
960. fear
961. workers
962. Washington
963. Greek
964. women
965. bought
966. led
967. march
968. northern
969. create
970. British
971. difficult
972. match
973. win
974. doesn't
975. steel
976. total
977. deal
978. determine
979. evening
980. nor
981. rope
982. cotton
983. apple
984. details
985. entire
986. corn
987. substances
988. smell
989. tools
990. conditions
991. cows
992. track
993. arrived
994. located
995. sir
996. seat
997. division
998. effect
999. underline
1000. view